To Lisa,

Wishing you eve[...]
and joy in God's h[...]

Love,
Mrs. Hayhurst
April 8, 2001

"And then my heart with
pleasure fills,
And dances with the
daffodils."

William Wordsworth

Published simultaneously in 1998 by Exley Publications Ltd in Great Britain
and Exley Publications LLC in the USA.

12 11 10 9 8 7 6 5 4 3 2 1

ISBN 1-86187-097-3

Illustrations by Brian Grimwood.
Edited by Andrew Maxwell Hislop.
Quotations researched by Andrew Maxwell Hislop and Lincoln Exley.
Graphic Design by Acrobatix.
Concept Development by Lincoln Exley.

There is a broad range of cards and gifts featuring the artwork of
Brian Grimwood produced by Lincoln Exley Designs Ltd. For further details
please contact Lincoln Exley Designs, Suite 4, Kings Court, 153 High St.
Watford, Hertfordshire, WD1 2ER, UK.

Exley Publications Ltd 16 Chalk Hill, Watford, Herts. WD1 4BN, UK.
Exley Publications LLC 232 Madison Avenue, Suite 1206, NY 10016, USA.

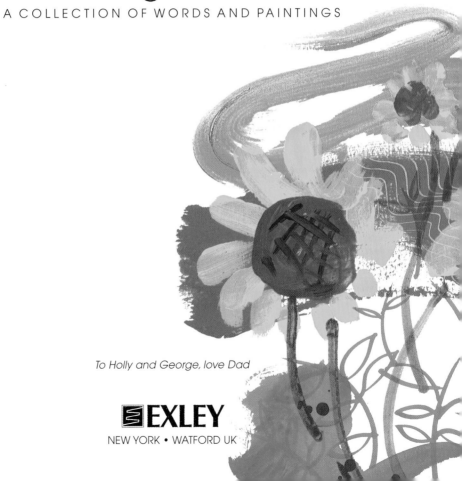

Earth Laughs in Flowers

A COLLECTION OF WORDS AND PAINTINGS

To Holly and George, love Dad

≋EXLEY

NEW YORK • WATFORD UK

Happiness is to hold flowers in both hands.
JAPANESE PROVERB

Many eyes go through the meadow but few see the flowers.
ENGLISH PROVERB

He who plants a garden, plants happiness.
CHINESE PROVERB

Into your garden you can walk
And with each plant and flower talk;
View all their glories, from each one
Raise some rare meditation.
Recount their natures, tell which are
Virtuous like you, as well as fair.

JOHN REA

Some people like to make
of life a garden, and to
walk only within its paths.
JAPANESE PROVERB

Don't hurry, don't worry.
You're only here for a short
visit. So be sure to stop and
smell the flowers.
WALTER HAGEN

Nobody sees a flower –
really – we haven't time.
GEORGIA O'KEEFE

Heaven Scent

The passions of men are incorporated with the

WILLIAM WORDSWORTH AND SAMUEL TAYLOR COLERIDGE

One touch of nature makes
the whole world kin.
WILLIAM SHAKESPEARE

In the Spring a livelier iris
changes on the burnish'd
dove;
In the Spring a young man's
fancy lightly turns to thoughts
of love.
ALFRED, LORD TENNYSON

beautiful and permanent forms of nature.

Fair daffodils, we weep to see
You haste away so soon:
As yet the early-rising sun
Has not attain'd his noon.
ROBERT HERRICK

For a breeze of morning moves,
And the planet of Love is on high,
Beginning to faint in the light that she loves
On a bed of daffodil sky.
ALFRED, LORD TENNYSON

And then my heart with pleasure fills, And dances with the daffodils.

WILLIAM WORDSWORTH

Nature is the art of God.
DANTE

The Amen of
Nature is always
a Flower.
OLIVER WENDELL HOLMES

The flowers are nature's jewels, with whose wealth she decks her summer beauty.

GEORGE CROLY

Our Summer made her light escape Into the Beautiful.

EMILY DICKINSON

Silence deep in summer's midst, sleep and dream.

EDITH SÖDERGRAN

Gather ye rosebuds while ye may,
Old Time is still a-flying.
And this same flower that smiles today,
Tomorrow will be dying.
ROBERT HERRICK

By the road,
In the hedgerow, a rose –
My horse ate it.
BASHO

But no one has plucked
the rose without the stab
of a thorn.
HAFIZ

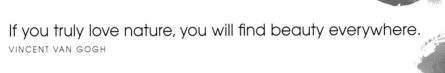

If you truly love nature, you will find beauty everywhere.
VINCENT VAN GOGH

Happy are those who see beauty in modest spots
where others see nothing.
CAMILLE PISSARRO

Can all your tap'stries, or your pictures, show
More beauties, than in herbs and flowers do grow?
ABRAHAM COWLEY

As the sun-flower turns on her god,
when he sets,
The same look which she turn'd
when he rose.
THOMAS MOORE

Earth's crammed with heaven.
ELIZABETH BARRETT BROWNING

Visibly through his garden
walketh God.
ROBERT BROWNING

Here is a heaven and earth,
beyond the world of men.

LI PO

A garden is a thing of beauty and a job forever.
ANON

Great god of little things
Look down upon my labors,
And make my little garden
A little better than my
neighbor's.
ANON

Perennials are the ones
that grow like weeds,
biennials are the ones
that die this year instead
of next, and hardy annuals
are the ones that never
come up at all.
KATHERINE WHITEHORN

Into the field of
Yellow flowers,
The red setting sun!

NATSUME SOSEKI

Heaven is under our feet
as well as over our heads.

HENRY DAVID THOREAU

Drows'd with the fume of poppies.

JOHN KEATS

But pleasures are like poppies spread –
You seize the flow'r, its bloom is shed.

ROBERT BURNS

Poppies

13

In the past, when the sun was setting,
God would appear to me
As a gardener
Walking down the pink horizon
And scattering water
Over the verdant world.

AHMAD 'ABD-AL MU'TÍ HÍJÁZÍ

The poetry of earth is never dead.
JOHN KEATS